THE FA SPOTTED EGG

A Traditional Collection

DOCTOR KNOW-IT-ALL

A Traditional Tale from Germany

ONCE there was a peasant, and he was very poor. All he had in the world was a patch of woodland, a two-wheeled cart, and a pair of oxen to pull it. From time to time, he chopped down some of his trees, cut them up into logs, and carted them into the village. If he was lucky enough to find a buyer, he would sell the wood for two dollars a load.

One day this peasant Fish (for that was his name) took his ox-cart full of wood to the village and sold it to a doctor. While Fish was standing at the open door waiting for his two dollars, a powerful smell of rich savory food reached his nostrils. Fish peeped in at the door. There was the doctor's dinner laid out on the table, all steaming and ready to eat: soup and roast, juicy vegetables, a frosted cake, and a dish of luscious

DOCTOR

fruit such as poor peasant Fish had never even laid eyes upon.

"Oh!" thought the poor man. "If I could only be a doctor too, and eat such heavenly dinners."

This set him thinking. After the doctor had given him the two dollars, the peasant lingered in the doorway twirling his cap this way and that; and at last he asked whether he might not learn to be a doctor too.

"Why not?" said the doctor. "It's easy enough."

"And how would one go about that, now?" asked Fish.

"First of all," said the doctor, "you must sell your two oxen and the cart. With that money you must buy some fine clothes; also a few medicine bottles, pills and pellets, salts, salves, and so on. Next you must get yourself a book—one of those ABC books will do, the kind with a rooster inside. And last of all, you must get a board with the words I AM DOCTOR KNOW-IT-ALL painted on it, and this you must nail over your door."

Fish did all this. Over his door hung the newly painted sign, in his room were shelves full of medicine bottles, on his table was the ABC book, while he himself was so fine and grand he felt like someone new. With his spectacles, his fine blue coat, his watch, and pointed beard, he really looked as though he knew it all. He was ready to start, but day after day went by and nothing happened. There he sat among his salves and pills with not a thing to do.

At last someone came, and a lord no less. This lord had been robbed of a big sum of money, and when he saw the sign, I AM DOCTOR KNOW-IT-ALL, he said to himself: "That's just the fellow I want. If he really knows it all, he will surely know who has stolen my money."

He knocked at the door, and when Fish heard him he straightened his spectacles, gave a pull at his watch chain,

put on his tall hat but took it off again, and at last he opened the door.

"So you are Doctor Know-It-All," said the rich lord.

"Oh, yes," said Fish.

"I want you to find my stolen money," said the lord. "Can you come with me now to my palace?"

"Yes, indeed," said Fish, "and my wife, Gretl—can she come too?"

"Certainly," said the lord; so they all stepped into his coach and drove off.

It was the dinner hour when they reached the lord's palace, so he invited Fish and Gretl to join him. They all sat down at the table, and when the first servant came in with a dish of soup, Fish whispered to his wife, "Look, Gretl, that is the first."

He meant that this was the first course being served, but the servant, who had overheard him, thought he meant this was the first thief who had stolen the lord's money. As he really was one of the thieves, he became worried; and when he reached the kitchen he said to the other servants, "Things will go ill with us, now that this Doctor Know-It-All is around here. Just think! As soon as he set eyes on me, he told his wife I was the first thief."

The other servants gasped in alarm; and when the bell tinkled for the next course, the second servant hardly had the courage to go into the dining room. But what could he do? It was his turn to serve. He tried to look innocent as he entered with a dish of steaming food, but Fish leaned over to his wife and whispered, "See, Gretl, that's the second."

He meant this was the second course, but the servant thought that he himself was meant, and his knees knocked together as he rushed back to the kitchen.

When the third servant came in with still another dish, it was the same. Fish nudged his wife, whispering: "And that, Gretl, is the third."

The third servant, his hair standing on end, set the dish on the table and dashed into the kitchen as fast as he could. Luckily the lord had noticed nothing. He had been too busy thinking up some way of putting Doctor Know-It-All to the test, and now he said, "Doctor, here is the fourth servant with a covered dish. If you really know it all, you should be able to guess what is in the dish."

Poor peasant Fish! How should he know what was in it?

He looked and looked at the covered dish; and at last, seeing he was caught, he said, "Oh, you poor Fish. You're done for!"

As luck would have it, there was a fish in the dish, and now the lord cried, "Well, well, Doctor, you've guessed it! Now I know you can find my stolen money too."

Poor peasant Fish! He was in a fix and no mistake about it. He was still racking his brains for something to say, when the fourth servant, who was just leaving the room, winked meaningly at him. Fish excused himself from the table and followed the servant into the kitchen. The servants, looking greatly frightened, said, "Oh, Doctor, you told your wife we were the thieves who stole milord's money, and it's true. But we'll give it all back to him, and we'll reward you besides, if you'll only promise not to tell on us."

Fish promised to keep their secret, and they showed him where the stolen money was hidden. When he returned to the dining room, he cleared his throat and stroked his beard, saying, "Hm, hm! So you want to know what's become of your money, milord. Hm, hm! Well, well! I'll have to consult my book about that."

He sat down and spread the ABC book on his knees. Then he put his spectacles on his nose; and, with an important air, he began to look for the picture of the rooster. Meanwhile the servants were curious to know whether the Doctor would really keep their secret, so the fifth servant was sent in to listen. He sneaked in on tiptoe and hid in the oven.

All this time, peasant Fish or Doctor Know-It-All (whichever you wish to call him) was still paging back and forth in his ABC book, but he couldn't find the picture of the rooster. At last he lost his temper and shouted, "You rascal! I know you're in there, and I'll find you yet."

The servant who was in hiding thought that he was meant. He jumped out of the oven, yelling, "Help! The man knows everything!"

Doctor Know-It-All, who had found the rooster at last, looked pleased, closed his ABC book, and cleared his throat again. "Hm, hm!" he said. "Yes. Well, well! And now as to your stolen money, milord. I can show you just where it is."

He led the lord to the place where the servant had hidden the money, saying, "You see, milord. Here it is, every penny of it."

The lord was pleased—so pleased, in fact, that he grabbed a big handful of gold, pressed it into Fish's hands, and said, "Well done, my good Doctor, and my undying thanks to you. I will spread your fame far and wide."

This he did too; and from that time on, Fish and his good wife Gretl lived in wealth and ease, had plenty of good food to eat, and rode about in a fine carriage.

The Old Woman and the Gourd

A Tale from Nepal

LONG, long ago, an old woman set out to visit her daughter, who lived with her husband a long way off.

By and by, she came to a thick forest, and there she met a fox. "Old woman," said the fox, "I have not eaten for ten days. You can go no farther. I am going to eat you up!"

"Be patient, dear fox," said the old woman. "I am going to visit my daughter, but I shall be coming back this way in a month's time. Let me go now please, because when I come back I'll be as fat as butter, and you will have a much better meal."

"A fat old woman would certainly make a better meal than a thin one," thought the fox, so he let her go.

She had not gone far when she met a tiger, the ferocious king of the forest. "Old woman," snarled the tiger, "I have not eaten for twenty days. You will make a good meal for me. Get ready to die."

"Please let me go, O King of Beasts," said the old woman. "You can eat me when I come back from visiting my daughter at the end of the month. I'll be fat and tasty by then, not thin and tough as I am now."

"A fat and tasty old woman would make a better meal than a thin and tough one," thought the tiger, so he let her go.

Before long she met the King of the Monkeys with all his tribe. "Good morning, old woman," he said, with a grin. "You have come just in time for lunch. It will give me much pleasure to eat you up."

"Be patient, O Lord of Monkeys," said the old woman. "I am on my way to visit my daughter, so please let me go. I am thin now, but when I come back in a month's time, I'll be fat and tasty."

But the King of Monkeys was not tricked so easily. He commanded his tribe of monkeys to surround the old woman. They shrieked and screamed, they snarled and hissed, and the young ones even scrambled onto her shoulders and jumped on her head.

She begged and implored them to let her go. But the King of Monkeys said, "I shall not believe that you are

really coming back unless you swear an oath by the Buddha!"

So the old woman had to swear an oath, and then the King of the Monkeys let her go on her way.

At long last she reached her daughter's house and stayed there happily. But the time flew by and soon came the end of the month.

Then she remembered what had happened with the animals, and she told her daughter all about it. They put their heads together and made a plan. The daughter picked two large gourds. One was a *lanka*, shaped like a bottle. The other was a *chinda*, shaped like a snake. Now the daughter was a clever woman. She put the old woman inside the *lanka* and told the

chinda to lead the way. So they went—the *chinda* zig-zagging like a snake, the *lanka* with the old woman inside rolling on its sides. By and by they came into the forest, where the monkeys, the tiger, and the fox were all waiting hungrily for the old woman.

The monkeys were the first to see them coming. They were very surprised at this strange procession—a snake that rattled and a bottle that rolled by itself.

"Make way for us," called the *chinda* loudly. "What do you mean by blocking our path?"

"We were just waiting for an old woman who promised to be our dinner," said the surprised King of Monkeys politely. "Did you see her, by any chance, as you came along?"

"What would we want with an old woman?" said the *chinda* haughtily. "Out of our way!" And the *chinda* and the *lanka* rattled on.

Soon they came to the place where the tiger was waiting. This time, he was ready to pounce on the old woman as soon as he saw her. First he heard a strange rattling sound, then he saw the *chinda* zig-zagging toward him. After the *chinda* came the rolling *lanka*.

"Make way for us!" shouted the *chinda*. The surprised tiger stepped out of the way, then suddenly he remembered. "Oh, have you seen the old woman who promised to be my dinner?" he asked.

"What would we want with an old woman?" said the *chinda* haughtily. "Out of our way!" And the *chinda* and the *lanka* rattled on.

By now the fox had heard about the strange procession rattling through the forest, and he was very suspicious. So he put a sharp-edged stone in the middle of the pathway. Then he hid behind a tree and waited.

Soon the *chinda* and *lanka* came rolling along at great speed. The old woman was chuckling to herself at the clever way she had tricked the monkeys and the tiger.

"Crack!" The *lanka* hit the sharp-edged stone and split from top to bottom. The old woman was thrown out onto the path.

Now, when the monkeys and the tiger realized that they had been tricked by the old woman, they all began to chase her; and just as the fox was going to eat the old woman all by himself, the other animals came racing up.

The old woman knew that she had been caught this time, so she thought very fast. "It would be wise to roast me first," she said. "I will taste much better that way."

So the animals made a fire to roast her. "The fire must turn to ashes before it's ready, then I'll be cooked in no time," said the old woman.

When at last the fire turned to ashes, the old woman took a stone and sat on it in the middle of the heap of ashes. The animals thought that their meal would soon be ready, so they closed their eyes to say grace.

Quickly the old woman scooped up some of the ashes and threw them in the animals' faces. They coughed and spluttered and rubbed their eyes, but the old woman ran out of the forest as fast as her old legs would carry her.

The fox and the tiger and the King of Monkeys were furious. But although they searched hungrily for her all over the forest, they never ever saw her again.

The Fabulous Spotted Egg

An Old Tale of the Cheyenne Indians

THE Cheyenne Indians, who rode the plains of North America in the seventeenth and eighteenth centuries, had a strange custom. Whenever they came to a wide stretch of water—a lake or a river, perhaps—they would throw some food or tobacco in before they rode across. Nobody asked the Cheyennes why they did this, but then, of course, nobody asked the Cheyennes anything. If you met a Cheyenne, it was safer just to run away.

Well, there was a reason. It was contained in a tale told by the Cheyenne storytellers, a tale about a great river monster and two brothers who discovered a fabulous spotted egg.

The two brothers—their names aren't known, but we'll call them Elder and Younger—had managed to get themselves lost on the prairie. The horizon

made a great big circle all around them, and there was nothing to see except the grass, waving in the wind. The brothers had a little water, but they had no food.

They walked a few miles and they got hungrier and hungrier, and soon the rumble of their stomachs was accompanying the rustle of the wind. Then all of a sudden they came upon an egg just lying on the ground with no sign of a bird or a nest anywhere near.

"Well, that's a stroke of luck," Younger said. "Look at that egg. I bet it'll last the two of us a whole week."

"I'm not so sure," Elder growled. "It doesn't look too healthy

to me."

"What do you mean?" Younger cried. "It's just an egg."

But if it was just an egg, it was just a very peculiar egg. For a start it was bright green with red spots. Also it was enormous—much bigger than a chicken egg. Much bigger, in fact, than a chicken. And how had it gotten there? It was, after all, in the middle of the prairie.

"It looks magical to me," Elder said. "I say we don't touch it."

"Come on!" Younger replied. "It was probably laid by a bird or a turtle or something. Okay, so it's a funny color.

But I'm so hungry, I'd eat a green and red spotted horse!"

So while Elder watched, Younger lit a bonfire and roasted the egg. Then he cracked the shell and began to eat.

"You sure you don't want some?" he asked.

"No, thanks," Elder said.

"It's really good. You don't know what you're missing."

In fact, Younger was lying when he said that. The egg was hard and rubbery. The yolk was green, the same color as the shell, and the white wasn't white but a sort of pink. And it didn't taste like an egg should. It tasted of fish.

Now even as Younger ate he began to feel sick, but something made him go on eating. He couldn't stop. Faster and faster he spooned the egg down until it was all gone and only the shell was left.

"I hope you know what you're doing," Elder muttered.

The next morning, when they woke up, Younger was feeling really ill. His stomach was like a carnival merry-go-round, and his eyes were as big as ping-pong balls. Worst of all, he was really thirsty. He drank all the water in his bottle, but it could have been a thimbleful for all the good it did him. Elder looked at him and sighed.

"You look terrible," he said.

"I feel terrible," Younger agreed.

"You're green!"

"Green?"

"And you have red spots."

Younger stood up. "Let's go!" he said. "The sooner we find water the better. I need a drink."

They walked until sunset, by which time Younger's skin had gotten greener, and his spots had gotten redder. Also, all his hair had fallen out, and he seemed to be having trouble talking.

"Sssssay," he hissed. "Do you think I made a missssstake eating that egg?"

"I guess so, kid," Elder replied.

“I guesssss it was kind of sssssstupid. But I’ll feel better when I get to water. I really want a sssssswim.”

The next morning he was worse. His arms had somehow glued themselves to his sides, and his nose had dropped off. He was a vivid green and red, and his skin was slimy like a snake’s.

“I feel worssssse,” he moaned.

“You look worse,” Elder said.

“Water!”

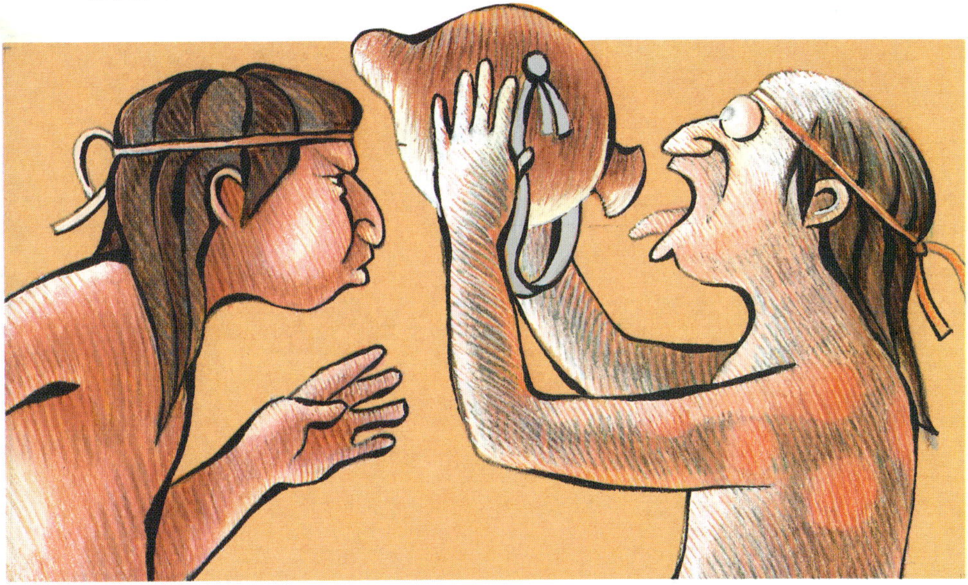

They reached water at sunset.

Younger, whose legs had almost melted into one another, decided that he would rather sleep in the river while Elder curled up on land beside a bonfire. Elder hadn’t eaten for five days now, and he was weak and tired. It didn’t take him long to fall asleep.

He was woken up by the sound of singing. He opened his eyes, and the first thing he saw was a great heap of fish lying on the bank, waiting to be cooked. Then he looked beyond, in the water, and saw his brother.

Except that it wasn't really his brother any more. The boy had become an enormous sea monster with huge teeth, scales, and a forked tail. He was swimming to and fro, stopping now and then to fork another fish with the point of his tail and flip it onto the bank.

"Hey, kid!" Elder called out. "How are you feeling today?"

"Fine!" Younger replied. "It'sssss not ssssso bad being a ssssssea sssssserpent. And I've caught a whole lot of fissssssh!"

"Thanks!" Elder said.

"Hey—lissssssten," Younger continued. "Don't you forget about me. I got you food, sssssso you get me food. I don't want to eat fissssssh all my life."

"I'll do that," Elder promised.

"And tobacco too. Just because I'm a monsssssster, it doesn't mean I can't sssssmoke!"

And that is why the Cheyennes always stopped and threw food or tobacco into the water before they crossed it (even when they were being chased). It was to keep the sea serpent singing.

THE FROG PRINCE

An Old, Old Tale from Germany

IN the old days, when making wishes was still some use, there lived a king who had three daughters. They were all beautiful, but the youngest was so beautiful that even the sun, who had seen so much, was surprised every time he shone on her face.

Not far from the king's palace, there grew a dark forest; and in the dark forest, under an old linden tree, there was a well. On very hot days, the youngest princess would go out into the forest and sit on the edge of the cool well. If she ever got bored, she would take out a golden ball, throw it up in the air, and catch it again. This golden ball was her favorite toy.

Now, one day it happened that the golden ball did not fall into her open hands, but bounced

into the water. The princess watched where it went, but the ball disappeared down the well, and the water was far too deep for anyone to see down to the bottom. So the princess began to cry and cry, and no one could comfort her. She was still weeping and wailing when someone called out to her, "What's the trouble, Princess? The way you are howling would melt a heart of stone!"

She looked around to see where the voice was coming from, and there she saw a frog poking his thick ugly head out of the water. "Oh, it's you, is it, Mr. Paddle-Splasher?" she said. "I'm crying because my golden ball has fallen into the water, if you must know!"

"Then don't cry any more," answered the frog. "I can help you—but what will you give me if I fish up the ball for you?"

"Oh, you dear, kind frog," said the princess. "You can have anything you want—my dresses, my pearls, and all my jewels—even my golden crown as well."

And the frog answered, "Dresses, pearls, jewels, crown? They'd be no use to me. But if you will love me and be my friend and playmate—and let me sit beside you at the table and eat out of your golden plate and drink out of your cup and sleep in your bed—I will climb down and bring you back your golden ball."

"Yes, yes," said the princess, "I'll promise you anything you want if only you'll bring me back my golden ball." But she thought, "The silly frog, what nonsense he talks. All he does is sit here and croak—he can't possibly be friends with real people."

As soon as the princess had made her promise, the frog ducked his head under the water, sank down, and soon came

paddling up again with the ball, which he threw onto the grass. The princess was overjoyed when she saw her beautiful toy again. She picked it up and ran off with it. "Wait for me," cried the frog. "Take me with you. I can't run so fast." But it did him no good, for the princess just ran home and forgot all about the poor frog, who had no choice but to climb back again into the well.

The next day as she was sitting at the table with the king and all his court, eating from her golden plate, there came a splish, splash, splosh up the marble stairs, then a knock on the door. A voice cried, "Princess, youngest Princess, let me in." She ran to see who it was, but when she opened

the door, there sat the frog. Quickly she slammed the door and sat down again at the table, but she was terribly frightened. The king saw how fast her heart was beating and said, "Why are you afraid, my child? Is there a giant at the door to take you away?"

"Oh, no," she answered. "It wasn't a giant, just a beastly frog."

"And what did he want from you?"

"Oh, dear father, when I was sitting by the well yesterday

playing with my golden ball, it fell into the water, and because I was crying so hard the frog brought it up for me. He made me promise to be his best friend and playmate, but I never thought that he would be able to get out of the well. Now he's here and wants to come inside with me."

And while she was speaking there was more knocking and a voice cried, "Youngest Princess, let me in. Have you forgotten what you said yesterday by the water's edge? Youngest Princess, let me in."

Then the king said, "If you made a promise, you must keep it. Go and let him in."

So she went and opened the door, and the frog hopped along at her feet until she reached her chair.

Then he sat down and called out, "Lift me up to you." The princess hesitated until the king ordered her to do it. But once the frog was on the chair, he wanted to be on the table; and when he sat on the table, he said, "Now push your golden plate nearer, so we can eat together." And she did, but it was plain that she did not like it.

The frog ate a good meal, but every mouthful stuck in the princess's throat. Finally the frog said, "I've had enough and I'm tired; now carry me up to your room, and we'll sleep side by side."

Then the princess began to cry. She was afraid of the cold frog, whom she couldn't bear to touch and who now wanted to sleep beside her. But the king was angry and said, "Never forget those who helped you."

So she picked him up between her finger and thumb, carried him upstairs, and dumped him in the corner. But when she was in her bed, he came hopping up and said, "I'm tired too, and I want to be comfortable like you. Pick me up, or I'll call your father." Now, this made her really

angry. She picked him up and hurled him against the wall as hard as she could. "Now you can go to sleep, you horrible little frog!"

As he fell to the ground he was a frog no longer, but a prince with kind and beautiful eyes, who, as her father wished, became her friend and husband. He told her how he had been bewitched and that nobody before this had been able to release him from the spell; and tomorrow they would go together to his kingdom.

Next morning, a coach came driving up with eight white horses all harnessed in golden chains and wearing white ostrich feathers on their heads. Behind stood the prince's faithful servant, Henry. Faithful Henry had been so sorrowful when the prince was turned into a frog that he thought his heart would break. But now as they drove away, Henry's heart was glad, and all the way to that distant kingdom he rejoiced that his master was free and happy again.

TIMIMOTO AND THE SILVER NEEDLE SWORD

An Old Japanese Story

TIMIMOTO was not much bigger than your thumb. He ate from a nutshell. He slept in a rice bowl. He rode in his father's pocket to see the village. He dangled from his mother's ear to see the river. And that's where he was, swinging like an earring, when they took the wash to the river bank one morning.

"Mother, it's time that I went off to see the world," Timimoto told her.

She wept and cried out, "My son, you are so small! People will trample you. Stay at home with your father and me."

No, he had to go. And that evening he sailed away in a rice-bowl boat, using chopsticks as oars. His mother's parting gift was a silver needle, a long slim needle as sharp as a sword.

Down the river...and down the river sped the rice bowl. The hungry, bulging eyes of a frog saw it swirl by. The frog sprang, open-mouthed, ready to swallow Timimoto in a gulp. *Swish!* He lunged. The silver needle-sword punctured the frog. It tumbled backward into the river and floated away.

Down the river...and down the river sped the rice bowl, to be washed ashore where a city dipped its streets into the shallows as if to wash its grimy feet.

Timimoto beached his boat and jumped ashore, ready to explore; ready for adventure.

People crowded the streets. Timimoto ducked and dodged, side-stepped and scuttled, skittered and jumped from the dangers of shuffling sandals and tramping boots. Then, as a crushing foot loomed alarmingly close, he sprang to the safety of the closest wheel on a passing ox-cart. He clung to the hub, jolted and shaken, until at last the cart came to a stop.

"Thanks for the ride!" he trilled to the Driver. His tiny voice sounded like the chirp of a cricket to the man who glanced about with interest, trying to locate the sound.

"I'm down here. Look at your toe!" shouted Timimoto. The Driver saw him now. Slowly, gently, carefully, he lifted Timimoto from the ground. Slowly, he balanced him on the lined palm of his old hand, looked at him in amazement, then said, "Whoever you are, Little One, you had best be getting home."

"But I've only just left home to see the world," explained Timimoto.

"Then find a safe crack where you can hide. As soon as the sun goes down, a great monster, the Ogre and none other, will walk the streets. Whoever he finds, he *eats*!"

"I'm not afraid of the Ogre."

"I am!" The Driver bowed his farewell and drove away, rattling and bouncing the cart in his haste.

Timimoto looked about and saw that the streets were emptying fast, as people hurried into doorways like scuttling beetles. When the sun dipped out of the sky, the streets were suddenly silent. Everyone had fled.

"Well, I'm here and here I'll stay," Timimoto shrugged. "Besides, I've never seen an Ogre."

"Who has never seen an Ogre?"

"The Great and Honorable Timimoto, and whatever Timimoto says is the truth!"

"Then Timimoto has spoken the truth for the last time!" snarled the Ogre, lunging from the shadows. His sword whistled. He swung and struck downward. *Crash!* He missed Timimoto, and his blade scored the pavement. Timimoto, nimble as a fly, flicked from the sword's path. Again it sliced the earth. Then the Ogre smote low, swinging the sword in slashing, widening arcs, each swipe closer to the ground...once, twice, ten, twenty times.

But Timimoto had already sprung away to the Ogre's foot, then jumped to a bent knee, flipped to an elbow, then to a shoulder, then with a great leap to his head, where he perched astride the Ogre's helmet. And he clung there while the Ogre slashed and hewed, chopped and sliced at his invisible enemy.

Little by little Timimoto pulled the silver needle-sword from his belt; then with his greatest strength, he thrust it down deep between the Ogre's eyes.

The monster roared. He reeled with pain. He crashed to the road and Timimoto fell with him, gripping the metal rim of the helmet. A great blast of air, the Ogre's dying breath, blew Timimoto clear of the mountainous body.

"No one need be afraid of the Ogre again!" Timimoto shouted, then searched about for his silver needle-sword. It was very troublesome to see, and when his eye did discover its glinting slimness, Timimoto gasped. It was shrinking; shrinking smaller and smaller. "Mercy me! It's almost too small to pick up!"

It was not the needle-sword which had dwindled in size. It was the same length and the same thickness. For the first time in many years, Timimoto was growing—upward and outward. His bones lengthened, his chest expanded to that of a six-year-old boy's, then a twelve-year-old lad's, a fourteen-year-old youth's, a twenty-year-old man's.

"Stop! Stop!" Timimoto clapped his hand on the top of his head. "I don't want to be Ogre-high!" Maybe he would have been, had not the Ogre sighed his last breath when Timimoto was just a fingernail taller than the men in that city, no more.

People poured out now, hurrying from houses and corners to congratulate him. They wanted him to stay as their Lord, but Timimoto was thinking fondly of his home. He stayed long enough to help clean out the Ogre's cave, which was a store of stolen treasure.

Timimoto departed with a cartload of gold and jewels to share with his people, but his most treasured possession was the silver needle-sword. It had slain the Ogre and released the strange power of magical growth, which had been spell-bound in the Ogre's breath.

CAP O' RUSHES

A Traditional Tale from England

NOW, there was once a very rich man, and he had three daughters. He thought he'd see how much they loved him, so he said to the first one, "How much do you love me, my dear?"

"Well," she said, "as much as my own life."

"That's good," said he.

So he said to the second, "How much do *you* love me, my dear?"

"Well," she said, "I love you better than all the world."

"That's good," said he.

So he said to the third daughter, "How much do *you* love me, my dear?"

"Oh, I love you as much as fresh meat loves salt."

Well, he was furious. "You don't love me at all," he said. "Out! Get out of my house at once and don't ever come back!"

So she went away. She walked on and on until she came to a bog, and there she plucked some rushes and made herself a cape to cover her fine clothes. Still she walked on and on until she came to a grand house.

"Do you want a servant?" she asked.

"No, we don't," they said.

"I haven't anywhere to go," she said. "I will work for you for nothing, and I will do any kind of work."

"Well," they said, "if you will wash the pots and scrape the saucepans, you may stay."

So she stayed there and washed the pots and scraped the saucepans and did all the dirty work. And the people there called her Cap o' Rushes because she would not tell them her name.

One evening, in a big house not far away there was to be a fine ball, and the servants were allowed to go and watch the guests dancing. Cap o' Rushes said she was too tired to go, so she stayed at home.

But after all the others had gone, she took off her cape of rushes, bathed herself, and went to the ball dressed in the clothes that she had worn when she left her own home.

One of the guests was her master's son. He fell in love with her as soon as he saw her and wouldn't dance with anyone else. But just before the end of the ball, Cap o' Rushes slipped away and reached home before all the other servants. When they got back she had put on her cape of rushes again and was pretending to be asleep.

The next morning they said to her, "You did miss out last night, Cap o' Rushes. There was the most beautiful lady you've ever seen at the ball. The young master couldn't take his eyes off her."

"Well," said Cap o' Rushes, "I wish I'd seen her."

"There's to be another dance this evening," they said. "Perhaps she'll be there again."

When the evening came, Cap o' Rushes said she was too

tired to go with them, just as she had the night before. But as soon as they were out of sight, she took off her cape of rushes again, bathed, and away she went to the dance.

The master's son was certainly glad to see her. He danced with no one else and never took his eyes off her. But again she managed to slip out and was home in bed before the others returned.

And the next morning, they said to her again, "Well, Cap o' Rushes, you should have been there to see the lady. The young master is certainly in love with her."

"Yes," said Cap o' Rushes, "I do wish I'd seen her."

"Well, there's a dance again this evening. You must come with us this time; she's sure to be there," they said. Again, when evening came, Cap o' Rushes said she was too tired to go, and no matter how hard they tried, they couldn't coax her to go with them. But as soon as they were gone, she pulled off her cape of rushes, bathed herself, and hurried off to the dance.

The master's son was delighted when he saw her. Again he would dance with no one else and couldn't stop looking at her. But when she wouldn't tell him her name or where she came from, he gave her a ring and told her he would die if he didn't see her again.

Before the dance was over, she slipped off again, and home she went. When the maids came home, she pretended to be asleep again with her cape of rushes on.

The next morning they said to her again, "Cap o' Rushes, you didn't come last night, and now you won't see the lady, for that's the end of the dances."

"I really would have liked to have seen her," she said.

The master's son tried to find out where the lady had gone, but no matter where he looked or whom he asked, he could not find out anything about her. He began to peak and pine and got worse and worse until he could not even get out of bed.

“Make some broth for the young master,” they said to the cook. “He’s dying of a broken heart.”

“Let me make it,” said Cap o’ Rushes.

At first the cook said, “No.” But then she agreed, and Cap o’ Rushes made the broth.

Just before the cook took it upstairs, Cap o’ Rushes slipped her ring into the bowl without the cook seeing.

When the young man had drunk the broth, there was the ring lying on the bottom of the bowl.

“Send for the cook,” he said. So up came the cook.

“Who made this broth?” he said.

“I did,” she said, because she was frightened.

“No, you didn’t,” said the young master. “Say who did, and no one will harm you.”

"Well, it was Cap o' Rushes."

"Send for her," he said. So up came Cap o' Rushes.

"Did you make my broth?" he said.

"Yes, I did," she said.

"And where did you get this ring?" he asked.

"From the person who gave it to me."

"Then who are you?" he asked.

"I'll show you," she said. And she took off the rushes and stood in all her own fine clothes."

Well, it didn't take long for him to ask her to marry him, and he got well very quickly! Invitations were sent to people from far and wide, for it was to be a very grand wedding, and Cap o' Rushes' father was invited. But before the wedding, she went to the cook and said, "I would like you to cook every single dish without a speck of salt."

"That will taste terrible!" said the cook.

"It doesn't matter. Just do as I say."

So the wedding day came, and after the ceremony they all sat down to the feast. When they began to taste the meat, no one could eat it, it tasted so horrible. But Cap o' Rushes' father tried first one dish and then another, and then he burst into tears.

"What's the matter?" said the master's son to him.

"I once had a daughter. And one day I asked her how much she loved me. 'As much as fresh meat loves salt,' she said. So I sent her away because I thought she didn't love me at all. Now I know she loved me best of all. And for all I know she may be dead now."

"No, she isn't, Father," said Cap o' Rushes. "Here I am." And she went over to him and hugged him. Then they finished the feast with much joy and lived happily ever after.

THE WHITE CRANE

A Traditional Tale from Japan

ONCE long ago in the cold high mountains of Japan, a woodcutter was pulling his load of logs home through the snow when he heard the sound of wings flapping wildly nearby. He looked behind him and saw a lovely white crane caught in a tangle of vines.

Quickly the old man left his load and went to the crane. He gently untangled the vines, loosened the wings and, stroking its soft feathers, set the bird free. The crane flapped its wings and, with a shrill cry, flew away into the distance.

That night when the old man and his wife were finishing their simple meal, they heard someone tapping on the door.

"Who can this be out in the snow on such a night?" said the old lady as she hurried to open the door.

Standing in the snow was a beautiful young girl.

"Come in, you poor dear," said the old lady. "Whatever are you doing out in weather like this so far from home?"

The girl bowed her head politely.

"I have no home, no family, and not even a name. Please may I stay with you until the morning?"

"Yes, of course, my dear. Come in and warm yourself by the fire," said the old lady.

They gave the girl a bowl of warm broth and a place to sleep near the fire. But the next morning the snow was still falling heavily; no one could travel in such weather.

That evening the old people said, "We have decided to offer you a home with us. If you will be our daughter, we will be your parents. We shall give you a name, *O-tsuru*—Miss Crane—for you are as beautiful and as graceful as a crane."

So O-tsuru became their daughter, and the small family lived together happily. O-tsuru sang and danced with the young people in the village, who were glad to have such a happy newcomer in their midst.

But for the old couple life was hard. The old man needed to cut more logs to sell in the market now that his family was larger, and the old lady patched and sewed to clothe them all.

One morning O-tsuru said, "My father and my mother, I should like to weave some cloth for you, but please do not come near me while I am working.

I must be alone in the loft or I cannot weave well."

"As you wish," said her parents, and they promised to keep away from the loft. They waited patiently as O-tsuru worked. They could hear the loom clattering hour after hour. At last O-tsuru came out carrying in her arms a bolt of exquisite silk cloth. "What wonderful cloth!" said the old couple together. "How did you make it so soft, and the colors so delicate?"

"Please do not ask me to explain how I did it," said O-tsuru. "My father, will you take it to the market and exchange it for gold? There will be enough to keep us in food and clothing until the end of winter, and you will not need to go out into the snow any longer."

So the old man took the cloth to the village. He found a merchant passing that way who, when he had looked at the cloth and felt its soft texture, said that he would gladly pay handsomely for it, since he had never seen its equal.

When the old man went home with the gold, his wife was amazed. "We have never ever seen so much gold before," she said. "How can we ever thank you, O-tsuru!"

O-tsuru was glad that she was able to make the old couple so happy, for she loved them as dearly as if they had been her real parents.

A long time later, O-tsuru said, "My father and my mother, I will go into the loft again to weave. Please remember what I asked you before. Do not open the door or look into the loft while I am at work."

"Of course not, dear child," the old man and old lady assured

her. This time the sound of the loom continued even longer than before. Many hours passed and still O-tsuru worked. "She will be exhausted," said the old lady.

The old couple became curious to know what O-tsuru was doing and why she was taking so long. They decided that it would do no harm just to peep into the loft. They crept quietly up the stairs and opened the door just a crack, but when they looked in, they both cried out together. There, seated in front of the loom, where they expected to see O-tsuru, was a beautiful white crane, plucking out its own feathers to weave into cloth.

As soon as it heard their cry, the crane began to disappear, and in its place O-tsuru stood.

"Oh, my dear parents," wept O-tsuru. "I cannot stay with you now since you have discovered my secret. I am the crane whom you rescued, dear father. I came here to repay you for saving my life, but now I must go. You have loved me and cared for me and I thank you for this. Farewell."

Even as she spoke these words, O-tsuru changed again into the tall white crane.

"Oh, please stay, O-tsuru," pleaded the old couple. But the crane was already flapping her wings. Slowly she sailed out into the darkening sky and disappeared.